MICHELLE
OBAMA
★ Mom-in-Chief ★

GROSSET & DUNLAP
Published by the Penguin Group
Penguin Group (USA) Inc., 375 Hudson Street, New York, New York 10014, USA
Penguin Group (Canada), 90 Eglinton Avenue East, Suite 700,
Toronto, Ontario M4P 2Y3, Canada
(a division of Pearson Penguin Canada Inc.)
Penguin Books Ltd., 80 Strand, London WC2R 0RL, England
Penguin Group Ireland, 25 St. Stephen's Green, Dublin 2, Ireland
(a division of Penguin Books Ltd.)
Penguin Group (Australia), 250 Camberwell Road, Camberwell, Victoria 3124, Australia
(a division of Pearson Australia Group Pty. Ltd.)
Penguin Books India Pvt. Ltd., 11 Community Centre, Panchsheel Park,
New Delhi—110 017, India
Penguin Group (NZ), 67 Apollo Drive, Rosedale, North Shore 0745, Auckland, New Zealand
(a division of Pearson New Zealand Ltd.)
Penguin Books (South Africa) (Pty.) Ltd., 24 Sturdee Avenue,
Rosebank, Johannesburg 2196, South Africa

Penguin Books Ltd., Registered Offices: 80 Strand, London WC2R 0RL, England

Photo credit: Cover: ©Bill Greenblatt/Polaris, © Frederic Cirou/Getty Images (background);
title: © AFP/Getty Images; pages 4-5: © Associated Press; page 8: © Polaris; page 16:
© Associated Press; page 17: © Associated Press; page 21: © Natalia Bratslavsky/iStockphoto;
page 22: © Polaris; page 23: © Denis Jr. Tangney/iStockphoto; page 26: © Susan Lapides/
Polaris; page 27: © Associated Press; pages 28-29: © Polaris; page 30: © Polaris; page 31:
© Polaris; page 32: © Getty Images; page 33: © Associated Press; page 35: © Associated Press;
page 36: © Associated Press; page 37: © Associated Press; page 39: © Associated Press; page 40:
© Associated Press; page 41: © Getty Images; page 43: © Associated Press; page 44: © Cristina
Ciochina/iStockphoto; page 48: © Getty Images

Library of Congress Cataloging-in-Publication Data is available.

ISBN 978-0-448-45256-2   10 9 8 7 6 5 4 3 2 1

MICHELLE OBAMA

★ Mom-in-Chief ★

By Roberta Edwards

Illustrated by Ken Call
with photographs

Grosset & Dunlap

On January 20, 2009, Barack Obama made history.

He became the first African-American president of the United States. On that

same winter day, his wife, Michelle Obama, also made history. She is now the first black First Lady of our country.

Like her husband, Michelle is smart
and good-looking . . . and very tall! (She
is almost six feet tall.) Like Barack, she
graduated from Harvard Law School.

They both say that their daughters,
Malia and Sasha, are "the light" of their
lives. They both enjoy spending time with
family and old friends.

But in most ways, they are very different. Barack likes to stay up late. Michelle loves to get up early—sometimes at the crack of dawn, she is already at the gym.

Barack is a dreamer. Even in kindergarten, Barack said he wanted to be president someday. Michelle is practical and down to earth. (Barack calls her his "rock.") Michelle never wanted to enter politics. She didn't ever dream of being the first lady.

Their childhoods were very different, too. Barack was born in Hawaii and as a young child lived for several years in Indonesia. Michelle, who was born on January 17, 1964, grew up in Chicago, Illinois. Until she went to college, she never lived anywhere else. Unlike Barack's parents who separated when Barack was only two, Michelle's parents had a strong and long marriage.

Michelle was taught to stand up for herself. Even as a very young child, she always knew her own mind. No one could push little Michelle Robinson around.

When she and her older brother, Craig,
played "office," he got to be the boss,
while Michelle was the secretary.

But Michelle never let him do anything!

The Robinsons were a loving and close-knit family.

Michelle's mother, Marian, stayed home to care for both children when they were young. Fraser, Michelle's father, worked for the city's water department.

As a young man, Fraser was struck with multiple sclerosis, a disease that slowly cripples people. Eventually he had to use two canes. Still Fraser never lost his sense of humor or his strong spirit. He was Michelle's hero, someone she never ever wanted to disappoint.

The Robinsons weren't poor, but they didn't have a lot of money. What the family enjoyed most was spending time together. On Saturday nights, the Robinsons loved to play Monopoly or Chinese checkers. Lots of aunts and uncles and cousins would stop by to visit.

In many ways the Robinsons were a lot like the happy TV families on *The Dick Van Dyke Show* and *The Brady Bunch*— shows that Michelle Obama still watches and loves today.

However, none of the families seen on TV in the 1960s were black.

The Robinsons lived in a brick bungalow on the South Side, an all-black neighborhood.

Neighborhoods in Chicago at that time were either white or black. Very few white people chose to live in black neighborhoods. In white areas, hardly anyone would sell a house to a black family.

The South Side of Chicago

President Lyndon Johnson signing the Civil Rights Act

The Civil Rights Act was passed in 1964, the same year Michelle Robinson was born. From then on, it was against the law to deny African Americans the same chances white people had for good homes, good jobs, and good schools.

Michelle's parents didn't want just *good* schools for Craig and Michelle. Only the *best* schools would do. Michelle, who was smart and hard-working, was accepted to Whitney M. Young Magnet High School. As a magnet school, it drew bright students, black and white, from all over Chicago. It was a long way from her home but worth the trip.

Friendly and well-liked, Michelle was in the National Honor Society and was treasurer of her senior class. She didn't mind working hard. However, it did bother her that Craig didn't have to work hard at all. He could watch TV or play basketball for hours and he would still get great grades on all his tests. That didn't seem fair!

When it came time to decide on a college, Michelle's parents encouraged her to apply to Princeton University in New Jersey. Craig was already a student there. Michelle thought, "I'm smarter than him! If he can get in, I can get in."

Michelle was right. And when Princeton accepted her, she decided to go.

Princeton was a different world for Michelle. In 1981, there were more than eleven hundred students in her freshman class. Only ninety-four were African Americans.

Michelle's roommate was a girl from the South. She was white. She and Michelle seemed to get along well, yet after a few months, the girl moved to another room.

Princeton University

Most of Michelle's friends were other African-American students. In a paper written in her final year, she said that Princeton made her much more aware of being black. She wrote, "I sometimes feel like a visitor on campus, as if I really don't belong."

Michelle Robinson, Princeton graduate

Harvard University

From Princeton, Michelle went on to Harvard Law School. After three years, she graduated. Now she had degrees from two of the top universities in the country.

Michelle returned to Chicago. A famous law firm hired her. She was making a lot of money. Yet Michelle's success was not making her happy.

Every day in her neighborhood, she saw people still struggling to get by. She wanted to do something to help them.

It was at this point that she met Barack Obama. He had a summer job at the same law firm. At first, they were just friends. Michelle even tried to fix up her friends with Barack.

Michelle and Barack Obama at their 1992 wedding

But by the end of the summer they had fallen in love. In 1992, they were married.

Michelle admired Barack for wanting to
help people in need. After law school, he
worked in Chicago as a civil rights lawyer.
If somebody had been treated unfairly
by a landlord or at a job, Barack would
take the case to court.

In 1991, Michelle's father died. It was
a terrible loss for her. His death also
made her aware of how short life is. She
has said, "If what you're doing doesn't
bring you joy every single day, what's the
point?"

She left the law firm to work for the
mayor of Chicago.

Later, she worked at a leadership training program for young adults and, after that, for the University of Chicago Hospitals. She helped doctors and local clinics provide health care for poor patients.

In 1998, Barack and Michelle's first daughter, Malia, was born. Sasha (short for Natasha) was born in 2001. Michelle has said that her girls are the first thing she thinks about when she wakes up every morning and the last thing she thinks about before she goes to sleep. Michelle never misses dance recitals or parent-teacher meetings. Barack also does his best to be there whenever he can.

Michelle is a fun mom, too. Not many people know this, but Michelle Obama is a great hula-hooper! She can even go from standing to kneeling and still keep that hula-hoop spinning.

Michelle believes that a family needs to spend time together, just the way her family did when she was growing up.

But in 1996 when Barack was elected to the state senate in Illinois, that became harder. The state senate meets in Springfield, one hundred and fifty miles away from Chicago. For eight years, Barack commuted between the two cities.

Barack is sworn in to the US Senate

Then in November 2004, at age 43, Barack won the race for the US senator from Illinois. Out of one hundred United States senators, he was among the very youngest—and the only African American.

Being a senator meant working in Washington, D.C. Many families of senators move to Washington. But Michelle didn't want to uproot her daughters. Neither did Barack. Malia and Sasha were happy at their school; they had lots of friends. And their grandma—Michelle's mother—lived close by. The Obamas stayed in Chicago. This meant Barack could only spend part of each week with his family.

Michelle was a working mom. And with Barack gone much of the time, it was up to Michelle to make sure the girls got to tennis lessons, practiced piano, and did their homework. She was the one who tucked them into bed and kissed them good night most evenings.

When he was home, Barack tried his best to help out. One time he offered to go shopping for goody bags for one of the girls' birthday parties. But Michelle knew Barack wouldn't have a clue what to buy. He didn't even know that you needed different stuff for girls and boys.

Malia and Sasha adore their father. He takes them roller-skating. He has read them all the *Harry Potter* books. Yet once Malia had to explain that a normal dad wouldn't shake hands with her friends. That's what senators did. A normal dad would wave and say "hi."

Of course, to the outside world, Barack Obama was a superstar—a Democrat with a bright future.

In 2007 he began campaigning to be president. He spoke to people all over the country. So did Michelle.

Michelle drew big crowds, perhaps because she is so warm and friendly. But a few times her openness caused problems. In one speech she said that Barack's campaign made her proud of America for the first time in her life. Many people didn't like that remark. It sounded like a put-down, although Michelle had only meant that she was prouder than ever.

Still, Michelle kept on campaigning. It took up more and more of her time. She had to leave her job. Often, her mother had to stay with the girls. But Michelle had a rule: On any trip, she was never away from her daughters for more than one night.

On November 4, 2008, Barack Obama won the election for president. It was truly a historic moment. Yet only three days later, he dropped the girls off at school, just like any other dad.

Suddenly the Obamas were famous all over the world. On January 20, 2009, right after Barack was sworn in as president, they became America's newest First Family.

They moved into the White House, the most famous home in America. There is a private theater, bowling alley, swimming pool, and chef to cook special treats for the girls and their friends.

But what excited Malia and Sasha more than anything? Getting a puppy!

Before the election, their parents had promised that—win or lose—the girls would get a dog.

Like other First Ladies, Michelle Obama
will work for causes that have special
meaning for her. Having been a working
mom, she hopes to help other women
juggle the demands of a job and a family.

Above anything, however, she wants
her daughters' lives to stay happy and
as normal as possible. The family will do
the things they have always enjoyed—
watching movies and playing Twister and
Scrabble.

And Michelle will continue to do what she enjoys most—being Mom-in-Chief!